The Ivy Leag

A Stanford Student's

Admissions

Winston Lowe

Table of Contents

About the Author

Winston was born in Saint Paul, Minnesota to two very poor, very stressed (but incredibly hardworking) graduate students. His family then moved around the Midwest until finally deciding to live in a small town in Wisconsin, where Winston attended high school. With no exceptional talent and after receiving rejection from the local Gifted and Talented program, it was during high school that he (possibly foolishly) set his sights on attending an Ivy League university one day. Fast forward four years down the road and he was accepted into nearly all of the Ivy Leagues and elite schools he applied to, such as Stanford, Yale, UCLA, and UC Berkeley. If a boy like himself with no particular knack for anything could make it into these types of schools, he figured anyone else could too. Thus, he wrote this book.

Introduction

So you want to make it to the Ivies? You want to experience the lectures of some of the most accomplished professors on the planet, have access to state-of-the-art research facilities, meet some of the brightest young adults from around the globe, and have your name attached to one of the most reputable institutions in the history of mankind? But do you not feel smart enough, unique enough, or simply talented enough to make it? Well, you've found the right book. Okay, that was cheesy. But seriously, if what I just described sounds like you, then stop looking elsewhere because this book is what you've been searching for. There is a notion that high school students who are accepted into Ivy League universities have to be the best in the nation or world at what they do, have discovered the cure for a previously incurable disease of some sort, or inherent geniuses. This, however, is simply not the case. I know first-hand that you don't need to be the best at something, you don't need to have done world-class research, and you definitely don't need to be some sort of genius to be accepted into these elite institutions. How do I know this, you ask? Well, I, myself, was a student just like you: fairly adept at most activities, but stellar in none. And you know what? I was accepted into not only my current institution of attendance, Stanford University, but into Yale, UCLA, and UC Berkeley also. Thus, this is why I am writing this book; I want to open the eyes of students like you. With Stanford University setting a new record low with a 4.7% acceptance rate in 2016, and most other elite colleges close behind, the need for a clear and effective guide for high schoolers is higher than ever. I want to show that you, my fellow 'non-genius' student, can too be accepted into the college of your wildest dreams.

This book is written from a very real and straightforward perspective. This is the perspective of a very recent high school graduate with no unique talents who strived to one day attend an elite university and got accepted into many. Sure, there are other sources out there with information about how to get accepted into elite colleges. Some of these sources have even conducted their own studies to support their information or claim to be "professional admissions consultants". While these sources may cite more statistical research than I do, what these sources are lacking is personal, real-life experience. I personally just went through high school not too long ago, and I understand how the system works and all of the ways that you can take advantage of it.

This book is tailored to young teenagers who go to public or private high schools (and anything in between) in America. Thus, I will not be writing with fancy words or overly complex ideas; I want this book to be as simple and truthful as possible. Ideally, you should simply read the book as a conversation between you (the reader) and me (the author). I will lay out a broken-down, step-by-step guide for you to follow so you can get yourself into the university of your dreams. Be sure to notice, however, that I said "so *you* can get yourself into the university of your dreams." Ultimately, your success comes down to how badly you want it and what you are willing to do for the sake of your goals. You would get the most out of this book if you were in eighth or ninth grade and seriously apply the advice that I give you all the way through high school from start to finish. However, you do not need to be in this age group to find this book useful. If you are in tenth, eleventh, or even twelfth grade there is still much you could learn from this guide, and it's never too late to start. Unless you already applied of course then you may want to put this book down. Anyways, the first few chapters of this book are split into the four years of your high school career and will tell you what you should specifically be doing during that year to improve your chances of getting accepted. The following chapters provide in-depth information about certain steps of the admissions process, such as what to do during your summers and how to write your application essays.

Finally, thank you for choosing this book. I am glad you have taken the first step to getting into the college of your dreams. I cannot guarantee success for you, but if you follow my steps, work your absolute hardest, and believe in yourself, you will likely not be disappointed.

Chapter 1: Why do YOU want to go?

Before we jump into things, I need to set a few things straight. The first being that you do not need to attend an elite college or Ivy League university to be successful in life. Let me repeat that, and just let it sink in this time: you *do not* need to attend an elite university to be a successful individual. If your main reason for attending an elite university is because you think it will grant you career or material success in the future than you need to rethink your reasons. Attending an elite university will allow you to access many new opportunities and open a myriad of doors, but what it will not do is ensure future success.

There have been many successful people who have not gone to Ivy League universities. In fact, I would argue that most of the people that American society generally deems successful did not even attend Harvard, Stanford, Yale, or other schools of the same caliber. Of the top one hundred C.E.O.s of Fortune 500 companies, only thirty-three attended an Ivy League college as of 2016. This means the vast majority of those C.E.O.s made it to where they are despite not attending any type of elite institution. I am not going to pretend to know exactly the cause for this correlation, but I can confidently speculate some reasons for this occurrence. First, when employers hire, they don't simply look for where the applicant attended school. Most employers look for work experience above all else. This hiring method makes sense, because someone is ultimately hired for how well they work, not how well they did in school. Second, success is influenced much more by one's interpersonal skills, ambition, and creativity rather than place of undergraduate attendance. An intelligent and capable student who decides to attend a state college or lesser-known private university can become equally (or even more) successful than his or her Ivy League counterpart.

Why even go to an elite institution then, you wonder, if it doesn't lead to automatic success in the future? Although attending a highly ranked, highly competitive school will not guarantee success in the future, what it will do is highly *increase* the probability of future success. Which, if you think about it, is all one can really do in life. No actions taken in life can guarantee success, but can only increase the likelihood of success happening. Going to an Ivy League school helps with future success because of a variety of reasons. One reason being the access to cutting-edge and up-to-date technologies and methods. These elite schools act as a hub for the newest and most powerful technology. Simply having access to so much state-of-the-art tech will allow you to pursue projects you could not anywhere else and learn in ways that you would have never expected. Another reason to go to an elite university is to be taught by some of the most accomplished and knowledgeable professors in the world. Elite universities draw world-class professors like these because of their endowment (the money/financial assets that are donated to the universities), which these professors will utilize for their own research. Thus, a cycle of success is created. The hefty endowment brings in world-class professors, the renowned professors attract bright students, the bright students utilize their education to become successful, the students then give back to the university they attended, and the cycle rinses and repeats itself over again. By being a part of this cycle of achievement, you are not only helping yourself, but the university and the field of research itself too. A third reason to attend an elite school is to surround yourself with thousands of other bright and incredibly motivated students. While it definitely will be a change going from the most accomplished person you know in your hometown, to a near-nobody at an elite university, the change opens many doors that simply would not have been there before. Being around people who are equally as motivated and sharp as you may be daunting, but it also allows for collaboration. The old saying 'two minds are better than one' certainly does ring true, and having an effective partnership can amount to levels of success that working alone would have never been able to reach. In fact, some of the most renowned and powerful companies in America today were formed by partners who met at an elite university. One example being the co-founders of Google, Larry Page and Sergey Brin, who first met at Stanford. Another example of an ultra-successful company being built by people who met at an elite university is Facebook, whose founders met at Harvard. Aside from what I've discussed so far, another reason to attend an elite university is simply because of the brand name that comes along with it. American society is one that values designer labels, and attending a university like Harvard or Stanford establishes a powerful label that sticks with you for life. It's a label that says: "Hey, hire me and/or trust me. I can get into a college this selective, and I likely can do whatever the current task at hand is too." By going to an elite university and attaching yourself to such a powerful marker of ability, finding jobs and gaining overall respect throughout life will come easier (not *easily*, just *easier*).

So I know we haven't gotten to the real meat of what you bought this book for yet, but the items we just went over needed to be established before anything else. I hope after reading this initial chapter that you truly think about whether or not you actually want to attend an elite college, and why. The journey to an elite institution is not easy by any means, and it will most likely be one of the most arduous goals you have ever undertaken. You will have to push yourself to your limits. If these demands are things you don't think you can muster, then put down this book now and stop wasting your time. It's okay, my feelings won't be hurt. But if you feel like you are going for the right, personal reasons and think you want it bad enough, then please, I urge you to continue reading.

Chapter 2: Beginning Your Journey (Freshman Year)

Now it's time to get to what we've all been waiting for, the actual guide itself. Ideally, your journey to the Ivy Leagues should truly begin in your freshman year of high school. Although most of your activities won't start until sophomore year, it's good to know what you will need to be doing and/or looking out for from early on. Later on in the book, I will lay out an example of a few students' year-by-year activities, showing and describing what they did each year of high school. But for now, we'll just take a broader look of what the initial steps during your freshman year should look like.

Coming into high school can be nerve-wracking and leave you feeling quite clueless. The environment is completely new, you don't know your way around, and you know nearly nothing about how the school functions. By how the school functions, I mean how the school grades, how to join clubs, how to run for leadership positions in the clubs, which classes to take or not take, how much leeway you have with your class schedule, etc. There are tons of big and little details that you simply cannot know until you've been in the environment for a long enough time. This is why you should spend your first year in high school simply getting acquainted to the new environment, putting forth your full effort into your classes, and scoping out clubs/groups that you think you'd like to join in the future. This initial year acts as a buffer between middle school and the true experience of high school. But do not make the mistake of simply coasting by. This year must be spent trying your hardest in classes, researching which classes you need to take the next year (sophomore year) to eventually be top of your class, understanding how the grading system works at your school (so you can eventually use it to your advantage later on), and keeping your eyes peeled for potential clubs/groups/activities that match your own interests. You should try to be involved with one activity during your freshman year and then keep on the lookout for two to three different activities you could become involved with the next four years. When scoping out groups to join in the future, take into account what you are good at naturally, what you enjoy, who is already in the group, and what you want to become better at. Try to make a mental and/or written list with these categories at the top and the clubs that would fit under them. Also, although almost all of your high school achievements will not be accomplished during this year (besides getting good grades), the year is still pivotal in the whole scheme of things. So, once again, do not slack. In fact, throughout the whole four years of high school you shouldn't slack. Remember, someone else is working just as hard (or harder) than you to achieve the exact same spot that you want in the school of your dreams.

Also, another way your freshman year should be spent is networking with the other students in your grade. By networking, I mean trying to have laid-back, casual conversations with as many people in your grade as possible. You should do this because it builds your reputation and shows other students that you are a likable person (hopefully). Now, I normally don't endorse caring too much about what one's peers think about oneself, but you have to care to a certain extent if you want to establish yourself as a leader one day. Which, in fact, is what this networking stuff is all about. The other kids in your grade are going to be the kids who choose who their student-leaders will eventually be, and when they do, you want them to eventually choose you. Getting elected, however, takes time and effort. You have to try to talk to as many people as possible, and give off a good impression. But don't try too hard in these conversations, or people will be turned off by that. Try to show the right amount of interest, but not come off as if you want them to like you really badly. You want to become a leader in your school because college admissions officers love these types of kids. Applicants chosen by their peers to lead show lots of promise. Think about it. Peers would not elect someone that isn't trustworthy, and/or somewhat successful, right? Well, admissions officers know this and thus highly regard applicants who are student-elected leaders in their school. It's almost like the peers have already done a layer of filtering that the admissions officer won't have to do. Moreover, each year a university loses a certain number of student-leaders who had previously led university groups. These positions will eventually need filling, and students with past leadership experience can fill these vacant positions effectively. So, all in all, talk to as many people as you can starting your freshman year (ideally in middle school too--if possible), make sure to talk to people in a natural way, and plan on eventually running for a student-leadership position in your future years of high school.

Another thing you want to start during your freshman year is preparing for the SAT test or ACT test. You should pick one test to focus on so that all of your efforts can be honed in on improving at that specific test. Hold on, don't freak out now, though. What I want you to do is fairly simple and painless. First, just go out and buy an official SAT study book from the College Board or an official ACT study book. It is crucial that you make sure the study books are *official,* and not made by a company that doesn't create the actual test itself. This is important because textbook companies cannot replicate the same types of test questions like an official book can, and when practicing with test questions you will need to be using questions that are directly from the creators of the test themselves. Which is exactly what I want you to do for now, practice test questions and sections. Each week you should have 2 to 3 sessions where you sit down and run through practice sections for the test of your choice. These sessions should last about an hour long, and be done with laser-like focus. Not one hour of going through the motions, getting distracted, and not really trying, but one hour of pure focus. You can start off by just answering the questions as best as you can, with no timer at all. Eventually, however, you want to move to timed tests. Going through practice sections from these standardized tests since freshman year is extremely beneficial. Once you finish taking the practice section like you would a real test, check the answers and explanations either provided online or in the back of the book. If you see any incorrect answers that you marked, analyze and understand the explanation for the correct answer. The early and constant exposure will acclimate you to the types of questions and format of the test, which is super helpful when taking the actual test. Nearing the end of the year, you should already have a firm grasp on what types of questions to expect (and you aren't even a sophomore yet!).

I know that earlier I said you don't need to worry about joining clubs or participating in activities, but you really should be in one activity during your freshman year. And honestly, it shouldn't be that difficult to find an activity to be in because it can be virtually anything. Just make sure that it is an activity that you enjoy and are willing to participate in for all four years of high school. The activity could be anything; it could be a sport, debate, computer club, volunteering, yearbook design group, you name it. The reason why you want to at least be involved in one activity is to show the college admissions officers that you can be committed. So just choose something you've preferably done for a while already (so you know you have the ability to commit to it), something that you enjoy doing, and something you can see yourself doing for the next four years to come. This portion of advice isn't absolutely crucial for elite college admissions, but it is extremely beneficial.

There's also another action you can take during your freshman year to help you for the rest of your high school years. If you can, talk with your school counselor about your goals. You should be able to schedule a meeting with your counselor through your school. Do so and let your counselor know about your goals. Tell them about how you want to get into [insert elite school of your choice here]. Letting your counselor know about your future academic goals is a good idea because that way they can help you along the way. Your counselor may or may not play a pivotal role in your high school career. Sometimes counselors can change class schedules for you, tell you about different opportunities, or write a strong referral letter for you. Either way, it is a good idea to get to know them a bit, foster a relationship over the next four years, and tell them about where you want to be headed after your senior year.

So, here is what you should be doing during your freshman year in a quick recap: acclimate yourself to the new school, try your hardest in your classes, learn which classes you will need to take in the future to be the top of your class, be on the look-out for clubs/groups/activities that you would want to participate in in the future, network and meet as many other students as possible, begin preparing for the SAT or ACT test, join one activity that you think you can commit to, and let your school counselor know about your goals.

Chapter 3: Let's Get Competitive (Sophomore Year)

So you made it past your first year, got situated, and have begun setting up yourself for success in the years to come. Awesome. Now, just keep the ball rolling. It's pivotal that you follow my recommendations during your sophomore year of high school. This year is an extremely unique one, it's almost like a window of opportunity that you won't ever get back. The reason why I describe it like that is because sophomore year is the year that's sandwiched between the academically easiest year of high school (freshman year) and the academically hardest year of high school (junior year). By the time you're a sophomore, you have become fairly acquainted with the high school you're at, but have not yet begun to take an extremely time-consuming course load (in other words, one made up of many AP classes). If your high school is like mine was, and most others are, the offering of AP/honor/advanced classes does not begin until junior year, with the exception of maybe one or two classes offered sophomore year. This means colleges technically won't penalize you for not taking challenging classes during your sophomore or freshman year because your school simply didn't allow you to yet! Colleges will penalize you, though, if they realize advanced courses were options that you did not take. Although academics won't be the highest priority for this year, you still must keep straight A's. What should your highest priority be then, you ask? Allow me to explain.

So if you followed my guide correctly, during your freshman year you should have found a few activities or groups that you'd like to join. Now is the time to join them.

You want to join at least two to three groups during your sophomore year of high school (in addition to keeping your membership in the first group from freshman year). Make sure these are groups that you actually want to be in, meaning activities that you enjoy/are good at/have friends in. Or it can be an activity that helps you improve a skill that you have a burning desire to work on. You basically just need to find a club that you can be committed to for the next three years.

When you first join these clubs it is perfectly okay to just be a dedicated member. You don't have to try to be a leader in the club just yet (I doubt many people would want an inexperienced sophomore running their club anyways). Your time to shine as a leader in the club will come during your junior and senior years. For now, be a diligent member of the club and go to all the meetings and activities that the group hosts. Learn as much as you can about the people in the club, advisors, and opportunities available through the club. Also be on the lookout for outlets to compete through the club. Many high school clubs offer a competition side of the club that is optional. If this is offered, you want to take advantage of it. Immerse yourself into competition. Of course, if the activity you joined is an athletic team, then competition is a requirement. When I talk about optional competition, I'm mostly referring to science, business, speech, and other similar types of clubs. I'm going to spend some time talking about competitions and why they are important now, so if the clubs you have joined don't offer a competition aspect then look into clubs that do offer it or don't pay attention to this next section.

So, now we're going to talk about competitions and why they are important. Let's pretend for the sake of example that you are extremely interested in robots. Thus, you join your high school's robotics club. The club has meetings every week and there you guys learn about building robots and the applications of artificial intelligence. You then learn that there are competitions available for high school students where they can build robots to compete against one another. You could just remain a local member of the school's club and not compete, but you decide not to do that. So you and the others in the club make a team and sign up for the competition. You go to the competition, do well, and receive recognition for your achievement. This is essentially the basic outline for what you will need to do for all of the clubs you are in. During your sophomore year, you should join a club (it doesn't have to be robotics), be a committed member, and then try competing in a competition through the club. This process does many things for your overall goal of getting into an Ivy League or elite university. For one, this gives you a head-start in joining clubs because most kids wait until junior year to start becoming involved anyways. This earlier involvement will make you look more committed, more passionate, and ultimately more desirable to admissions officers. The second reason why you need to follow this process sophomore year is because when you compete in clubs you show that you are passionate, dedicated, and actually *good* at what you are involved with. If you aren't good, practice until you are (seriously, it's that simple, but that's not the topic of this book). You need to compete and you need to win at these competitions to show admissions officers that you have a burning passion for this activity and are skilled at it. Admissions officers much prefer an applicant who has competed through a club, than one who has simply remained a basic member. I know plenty of students who claimed to just be "members" of groups on their college applications and got rejected from many of the higher-caliber schools they applied to. Being a member is not enough, you must compete if possible.

Although extracurricular involvement is a main priority for your sophomore year, you need to still be doing well in school. This means essentially straight A's or the highest marks possible in all of your classes. By now, you should also be on the advanced academic track for your school, if that is an option. Your classes should be honors, advanced, enriched, pre-AP, or whatever fancy name they call it at your school. For one, colleges want to see you take as rigorous of courses as you can through your specific high school. Secondly, taking an advanced schedule your sophomore year will open up the doors for many more AP classes your junior year because of class prerequisites. Most high schools only start offering AP classes to students during junior year, but if your high school offers AP classes for sophomores (or even freshman, I suppose) you should definitely take up the offer and take the AP classes. But since most high schools don't offer AP classes until junior year (including the one I went to), I am going to base this portion of the guide around that type of structure. Thus, your sophomore year should, academically speaking, be spent getting as high as grades as possible in as advanced courses as possible. If your school is like most, AP classes will be weighted more than regular classes. All this means is that an

'A' in an AP class raises your G.P.A. more than an 'A' from a non-AP class. This is one of the reasons why you want to take advanced classes during your sophomore year: so you can take as many AP's as possible during your junior year, boost your G.P.A., and get to the top of your class. You do not, however, need to be the valedictorian (number one) of your class, just be in the top one to two percent. If you have a class of less than 300, try to be in the top one percent. If your class is larger than 300, it's fine to be in the top two percent. For the most part, it's safe to say that you will be competitive to Ivy League schools if you remain in the top one or two percent of your class. If your school does not rank kids, however, just try to get as perfect of grades as you can while balancing the other areas of your life such as extracurricular activities and relationships. I will elaborate more on the fine details of academics later since, for now, we are focusing on sophomore year. Moreover, when signing up for classes for your junior year, be aware of which ones are AP and which ones lead to AP classes down the road. If it seems like I'm emphasizing the importance of AP classes a lot, it's because they are important. If you do not show colleges that you desire to learn, want to be challenged, and can thrive in challenging classes, then they will not want you. One of the main way to show colleges all of these things, is through taking and excelling in many AP classes.

Another aspect of sophomore year that you need to keep in mind is preparing and possibly even taking standardized tests. First, continue your studying habits from freshman year. Keep practicing for thirty minutes to an hour for two to three days each week by going through practice sections from an official study book. Then, it is up to you whether or not you want to take an official ACT or SAT test during your sophomore year. I do highly recommend that you take a PSAT or PLAN test, however, as a sophomore. The PSAT is like a pre-SAT test that gives you exposure to the testing conditions of the actual SAT and gives you an opportunity to win a large scholarship completely based off of your test score. The PLAN test is like a pre-ACT test that is shorter in length and exposes you to the ACT's testing conditions. The PLAN test, however, cannot qualify you for the National Merit Scholarship like the PSAT can.

In a brief overview, your sophomore year should mainly be centered upon joining clubs, competing through those clubs, and winning the competitions. You should also, however, be enrolled in the most advanced courses you can be in and getting perfect or near-perfect grades in those classes. Sophomore year will be substantially busier than freshman year, but less stressful than junior year. Remember to keep your eyes on the prize, but also take the time to enjoy what you're doing.

Chapter 4: Time to Buckle-Down (Junior Year)

So, you've made it halfway. Don't get too cocky, because you still have a very tough half to conquer. The past year's focus did include academics, but it was not the most prioritized focus. Junior year's focus, however, is indeed academics. Depending on your natural skill-set, this may or may not be good news for you. Either way, it needs to be done. This is the year where you really show the admissions officers that you are academically qualified. This is theoretically the most important year, academically, for high school students because freshman and sophomore year classes are filled mostly with basic-level, required classes, and senior year's grades are not weighted as heavily when it comes to admissions. Of course, since you want to get into an elite school, however, you need to be putting forth full effort all four years. Anyways, the idea is that junior year is a very important year concerning your academics. You need to take challenging classes and succeed in them. Moreover, equally as important, you need start taking on leadership roles in the activities and groups that you're involved with. So, now that you have the basic overview, let's jump into the details.

If you followed my guide correctly, then your sophomore year should have been spent taking challenging classes that will set you up for academic success your junior year. This generally means that your sophomore year classes should have been pre-AP or advanced classes that lead to the AP class this year. Unless, you were able to take the AP class as a sophomore, then you obviously cannot take it as a junior.

This approach allows you to set yourself up for taking many AP classes and doing well in them.

Ideally, and in general terms, you want to sign up for at least 4 AP classes during your junior year, but it truly all depends on your school. Take more AP classes than what seems to be the average for students your grade level at your school, but do not over-do it. If students usually take 1 or 2 AP's during junior year, you need to take 4 or 5 AP's. If students usually take 3 or 4, you need to take 5 or 6. What it boils down to is staying well above the rest of the pack in terms of AP classes. Moreover, your classes should be diversified. What I mean by this is that you should not take all humanities AP classes or technical AP classes. Having a high amount of variety in your courses means taking some humanities class (English, history, art, etc.) along with some technical classes (math, chemistry, computer science, etc.). You do not want to be too heavily reliant on one branch of AP classes, as this will turn off admissions officers. This does not mean you need a perfectly even number of classes from both categories of academics, but just try not to lean too heavily in one direction.

With that information out of the way, you now know generally how many classes you should take and which ones. An essential aspect, however, is performing really, really well in your classes. This may seem obvious, but you need to bite and claw your way to getting an 'A' in your AP classes. Put forth your absolute full effort into your academics. Your junior year will push you harder than you have ever been pushed in school before. You will need to spend more time working on your classes than you have in the past and possibly more time than other students do. If you are having troubles with a class this means you should be asking the teacher many questions during class, going in before or after school to have the teacher further explain confusing concepts, doing extra practice problems that were not even assigned, and anything else that goes above and beyond what is expected. Remember, if you want to go to a better university than the other students in your class then you need to be putting in more effort than them as well.

While you strive for the highest grades during junior year, you also need to be keeping up with your extracurricular activities. This year, however, is not as heavy on the extracurriculars as sophomore year was. For your junior year, since your main focus is academics, extracurricular involvement will weaken slightly. Which should not hamper your overall resume, if you think about it. If you followed my guide, then you should have a wide variety of accolades and accomplishments from sophomore year. This allows you to spend less time acquiring extracurricular achievements during your junior year. The extra time that you now have will be invested into your academics.

Less involvement in your extracurricular activities does not mean you can slack off in them, however. Try your hardest not to quit something you already started and stick with clubs or groups to show commitment. Moreover, you can still compete in your clubs or activities during your junior year, just don't spend as much time practicing or training for them as you would have during your sophomore year.

Another highly important thing you need to do during your junior year, besides doing extremely well in your classes, is taking the ACT or SAT. You should take the test a total of two times during your junior year. I recommend taking it once in the first 2 months of the school year and then once again in the last 2 months. The first time around you should have had a decent amount of practice for the test because of the quick practice sessions you've been doing since freshman year. Do not stress too much about your first time, but do try your hardest. If you do not do well on the first test, you can always take it again. If you do well enough the first time, however, you save a lot of time in the future because you don't have to take it ever again. If the latter is your case, then you don't have to worry or prepare for the test anymore and now have more time to devote to other aspects of your application! Also, by the way, I'll take you through the process of trying to figure out where you should aim to score in a later chapter. For now, let's keep talking about testing during your junior year. Since you are most likely in the group that needs to take the test at least a second time (like most people), and the first score was not satisfactory, this next part will apply to you. I want you to take the SAT/ACT in the very beginning of your junior year so that you can prep for the second test you'll take later in the year.

The way that I want you to prep is by first doing well in your classes. By doing well in your classes you are actually learning (believe it or not) and developing your mathematical, critical reading, and writing skills. These are all sections tested on the SAT, and since AP classes are created by the same organization that makes the SAT, some of your AP classes may help improve your SAT test-taking abilities. Thus, doing well in your classes serves multiple purposes: boosts your G.P.A., prepares you for the SAT (if you choose it instead of the ACT), and of course helps you learn as well.

The second way I want you to prepare for your SAT or ACT is by practicing daily. Since your junior year will be very busy and full of homework and activities, your practice should be no longer than 30 to 45 minutes daily. When I say daily, however, I mean every single day of the year. This includes Fridays, Saturdays, and Sundays. You can of course take the holiday days off, however. This does not mean not studying for 2 weeks of winter-break, it just means not studying on the actual days of the holidays that you celebrate (Christmas, Thanksgiving, Hanukah, etc.). If you choose to study for the SAT, the way you should study is by taking one section of a practice test as you would the actual test. Take this section with the diligence and effort that you would if it were the real thing. Also since you have experience taking an actual test now and have practiced many times before, it's time to change up how you time yourself. For the SAT you should set your timer at 80% of the time that they say you are allowed for that section. For example, if you get 25 minutes for a section, you should set your timer for 20 minutes. This method of limiting yourself to 80% of the allotted time will make you much faster at taking the test over time. If you practice this 80% rule daily for multiple months, then you will not have a problem with timing on the test. After you finish each individual section for the official SAT book, you should go and check the answers and explanations for that section to see if yours match up. If they do not match up, examine the explanation that the College Board provides and try to understand the correct answer. Along with trying to understand the correct answer, you need to see what went wrong in your thinking processes. Was your estimating wrong? What part of the question led you down the wrong path? How can you fix your thinking process so that you don't make the same mistake next time? After you go through the section, correct your answers, and understand the explanations, you are done with that practice session for the day.

Your ACT practice will be in a similar manner, but since the length of the sections are different, your practice sessions will be slightly different than if you were to practice for the SAT. Since the sections of the ACT are longer than the sections of the SAT, you will conduct your practice sessions, if you choose to practice for the ACT, slightly differently. The ACT science and reading can be taken all at once and then graded all in the same session because of the shorter length of the sections. The ACT english sections will need to be broken up into separate halves that you work on during two different sessions. This strategy works because ACT english does not increase in difficulty as you progress through the sections, so they can be split into two halves by the number of questions. So, for the ACT english section split the section in half by questions, half the time limit allotted for the entire english section, take eighty percent of those halves, and go through the halves like you would any other practice session. ACT math, however, is a little more tricky. For the math section, you will need to just take the time to complete the section all in one sitting. Since the questions increase in difficulty as you go along, dividing the section in half would not be an effective strategy. Division in half by number of questions alone would make one half harder than the other, but force you to give equal amounts of time for both. This makes no sense and would be ineffective. So, since you can't circumvent this issue, just face it head on. Find the time out of your week to sit down for an hour and a half and take the ACT math section like you would any other practice session. Most students usually have this time during weekend mornings.

On a separate note, I recommend focusing on doing well on the SAT if you wish to gain admittance to an elite university. You can obviously get accepted with just the ACT or SAT, but if you look at which test most accepted students are taking, it's generally the SAT. You generally want to do what is commonly liked by the admissions officers, so doing well on the SAT would be more beneficial than doing well on the ACT. Although, whichever test you choose does not matter that much in the whole scheme of things. If you have a strong list of connected accomplishments, admissions officers will pay less attention to your standardized test history.

Another thing you need to keep an eye on during your junior year is keeping up with your activities outside of school. Although academics may come first during your junior year, you should avoid dropping more than one activity during this year (and if you do, you better have a darn good reason). You need to show commitment to the admissions officers; you can't just be another student that gets good grades and follows through with the motions. Keep up with your extracurricular activities that you have been doing in the past, and if you have the time, continue to succeed in them. Moreover, junior year is a great time to try to run for and acquire leadership positions in the activities that you are involved with. By the time junior year rolls around, you will have a good amount of experience with the group or activity, have established credibility, and be ready to lead. Holding some sort of leadership position in a group that you have been involved with for a while shows admissions officers passion, commitment, and your ability to lead. Since these are all qualities that make a person successful in the future, this is exactly what admissions officers want to see on an application.

Speaking of your application, you actually want to technically start 'working' on your application during your junior year as well. Now, I don't mean actually writing it, but just being aware of it. What you need to do is to make sure you develop relationships with your AP/advanced-course teachers during your junior and senior year. Elite schools generally require that you submit at least 2 teacher recommendations when applying, and you need these recommendations to be 'glowing hot' if you wish admission. What I mean by glowing hot, is that your teacher needs to write about you in a fashion that conveys to the college that she/he has the utmost respect for you and highly values you as a student. Each student will have different qualities, so obviously that cannot be the same, but generally each letter should emphasize your uniqueness and how much the teacher enjoys having you in the classroom.

The summer after junior year is also very important, but I will get to that later. I have dedicated a chapter to talking about how you should spend your summers.

In summary, during your junior year you should direct the bulk of your efforts into your academics. Take more challenging courses (AP, IB, etc.) than other students in your grade usually do and do well in those courses (mostly A's). Secondly, study for the SAT or ACT every single day. Go through practice sessions using the process described earlier in the chapter. Third, keep up with your extracurricular activities and run for leadership positions. If needed, you can put a little less time into your extracurricular activities, but try not to quit them. Also, run for leadership positions in your activities and groups. Lastly, keep a positive attitude. Junior year can be a very difficult year to overcome, but if you consistently try your best and believe in yourself, you will do great.

Chapter 5: The Home-Stretch (Senior Year)

Welcome to your final year of high school. You've come very far and you're almost to the finish line. Just one final push and you should be on your way to the college of your dreams. The first half or so of this year will be very busy, the second half, however, may provide some more time for relaxation. So, let's jump right in.

First, going into your senior year, you need to identify a list of universities that you are going to apply to. Keep in mind, that applying to a university takes a decent amount of time and money so make sure that the list is encompassing, but not excessive. Each university will usually charge a fee of around $50 to $100 just to apply. Seems over-the-top to me, but no one's going to stop them, and colleges love money, so it makes sense I suppose. Anyways, do not feel like you need to apply to all eight Ivy League schools, either. Just because a school is an Ivy League does not mean it would be the best fit for you. You need to look at the area surrounding the school, think about which major/programs you possibly want to go into, see if that school is known for or strong in that major/program, think about how you would react to the weather surrounding the school, whether or not you want to be close to home or far, if you want to experience a new part of the country or not, and what the student culture is like at the school. Also, do not eliminate applying to a school just because it isn't an Ivy League! There are many amazing schools that are not Ivies. All it means to be an Ivy League school anyways is that you have to be one of the first schools built in America. Being an Ivy League school, by definition, does not mean stellar academics or famous professors; it just means the school is really, really old. Schools founded later, such as Stanford, Berkeley, UCLA, MIT, Caltech, and Carnegie-Mellon are just as (or even more) amazing than many Ivy League schools. So, talk to people in your life about different universities, read online forums and conversations, and determine which schools you think would best fit you based off of the criteria I stated earlier. One thing I do know that can be applied to nearly every single elite school, is that if you followed my guide correctly, you should be able to gain acceptance to every single one you apply to. The criteria of elite schools is very similar across the board, and if you can get into one, chances are you can get into another one of similar caliber.

After you make your list of schools you want to apply to, you need to identify your number one choice. Pick the school that you think would give you the best opportunities for future career development in the field or fields you are interested in, the one that you think you would fit into the student culture/lifestyle best, and use whatever other criteria is important to you. This is the part where I can only do so much in guiding you, you need to pick for yourself what you think is best for you as an individual. Once you have identified your first choice school, you will want to apply to it through it's Early Decision program. Usually college's will have an Early Decision program that allows students to apply before the regular decision round even begins. The benefits of applying through this program, are that acceptance rates are usually much higher for the Early Decision round. Acceptance rates can increase as much as double or more of the regular acceptance rate. The drawback of applying early to a school is that many schools then restrict your from applying to other schools through an Early Decision program. This means you can usually only apply to one school through Early Decision, thus, this is why I had you identify your number one choice. Some schools even go on to require that you enroll at their school if you are accepted through their Early Decision program. You *must* check with the school you are applying Early Decision to and see their policies for the program. You do not want to break any agreements or get yourself into unwanted situations (legally or ethically). Either go to the school website to find the information you need to know about the Early Decision program, or call an employee at the university.

Once you have which school is your first choice figured out and how their Early Decision program works, you want to start writing your essays for that school as soon as the school releases the prompts for that application season. The schools will usually release their essay prompts sometime in August and through a website called www.commonapp.org. Create an account here and use it to check for released prompts. Sometimes schools will give students the option of choosing one of many prompts for a single question. Use this to your advantage and pick the one you think you could answer best. Once the prompts are released, first, read them thoroughly. Read them twice. Now take the time to think about what the questions are asking and some possible ways you could answer them. This may be a few days to 1 or 2 weeks for you. Make sure you write down all of your ideas, though. Whether it be written online, in a word document, or on paper, keep track of your ideas. If you have an iPhone, I recommend downloading an app called *Evernote* that allows you to take notes from wherever you are. This way when a great idea happens to pop into your head at a random moment, you always have your phone handy to write it down. A lot of kids make the mistake of writing their essays about what they think the admission's officers want to see in an applicant. This is because they have not even done the work necessary to even be qualified for a school of high caliber and are not confident in their skills. On the other hand, if you have put in the work and are confident in your accomplishments during high school, you will have no trouble writing about your true self. Everyone has a story and this is the time to share yours. Trust me. Even if you think you are the most boring and plain person, dig deep within yourself. There is no one else on this world that is exactly like you, so show that to the admissions officers. Even if you have had a 'typical, boring life experience', think about what you took away from your experiences. What perspectives did you gain or lose from your experiences? How did you look at your life experiences, in what lens or context? Your true self is your best self, so think your hardest about how you can show the admissions officers your passions, personality, motivations, dreams, and inner feelings.

Now that you have been letting the prompts marinate in your mind for a while, it's time to finally start writing. Although you will usually have to write multiple essays for multiple prompts to just apply to one school, it does not really matter which prompt you decide to write first. I do, however, recommend that you take on the biggest essay (largest maximum word count) first because it is likely the most important to the college admissions officers and will likely take the most time to completely write. The essays that have the largest amount of words often are read with the most weight, because this is where the admission's office is giving you the most space to explain who you are. Thus, although you don't have to, you should start with the largest essay first and work your way to the smallest essays (by max word count). The method that works best for writing your essays is a write, read, edit, and repeat process. You will follow this three-step process many times, often just to write one essay. Since you are beginning to write your essay in the summer, however, this should leave you enough time to make many drafts and revisions without feeling rushed for time.

Now, on to the topic of the actual writing. When you begin writing your first essay, you should find a day where you do not have much else to do. Sit down at your computer in a relaxed state of mind. People often write their best when they do not feel rushed or stressed, so try to avoid these feelings during your writing sessions (you should probably avoid them outside of your writing sessions too, but this isn't really an emotional advice book). As you begin writing, do not worry about the word count yet. However, do be reasonable about the word count and do not write too far above the word count limit. If your word count is beginning to go over 300% of the max word count for that essay, it may be time to rethink what you are writing. For example, for a 650 word-limit essay, this means if your essay is starting to surpass 1,950 words, you should think about condensing the topics you are writing about. However, for most kids, this will not be a problem. If you're like most kids, as you write your essay just freely write about the topics you wish and worry about condensing once you're finished writing. After you have your essay completely written out, go over it for any grammatical errors and remove or add any sections. Now, think about someone who knows you very well, someone you trust and can confide in (a parent, teacher, grandparent, uncle, friend, cousin, boyfriend, etc). Go hand this person your first draft, along with the prompt you answered. Allow this trusted individual to read your essay and tell them to let you know what they think about how you answered the question. Have them focus on whether or not the way you answered the question is true to who you are, and what they think of the topics you chose to write about. Their critique can be on the grammar of your essay, but it should mostly deal with the ideological aspects of your essay. Moreover, have them write down their critiques and advice for you, so that you can easily reference it later. This is why they need to know you very well. Once they return your essay along with their critiques, really allow them to speak their mind. Do not get angry at their critiques and be patient with them. However, do not also take what they say without a second thought. Use their advice as just that: advice, not command. Thus, you should tell them you appreciate their advice, ponder what they said, and only make changes to your essay if need be.

As you make changes to your essay and write your second draft, save a copy of the unedited version before you make any new edits. So before you edit a document called 'college.essay', name it 'college.essay.1', save it, edit the document, and save the edited document as 'college.essay.2'.

Of course, you don't need to use the name I chose, this was just as example. You do, however, need to follow the process of numbering your essay versions and keeping old versions of your essay. This allows you to not worry about forever erasing any good ideas and frees your mind to be more creative. When you write your second draft, seriously take into account what critiques the person had (especially ones about your ideas/topic). Make any changes that you deem necessary. The rest of the essay writing process will look similar to these initial steps. Write a draft, revise it, show it to someone you trust, analyze their critiques, make necessary changes, and save the new draft. If you have a close relationship with the person, they might not mind reading and critiquing every single draft for you. However, if you aren't as close with your chosen person or they are busy, you might want to only show them every couple of drafts. To truly write a strong essay that shows admissions officers who you are, you would need to draft your essay at *least* eight to ten times. This may seem like a lot of drafts, but when you have an amazing application essay that shows the core of who you are, it will all be worth it. As you write your essay it can also be a good idea to get more than one person to review it, if possible. I have found that two people total is the perfect amount of people to review your essay. Three or more and it will be difficult to maintain your own voice while managing all of their opinions. Two people, however, allows for multiple perspectives, but stays manageable for you. Of course, nothing crazy will happen if you talk to three people or more, but most of the time two is enough.

Repeat this process for all of your other essays until you have none left to write. For your smaller essays (ones less than 250 word max), though, you don't have to write so many drafts. Feel free to half the amount of drafts to three to five for these smaller ones. The most important thing to remember about the essays, however, are to write about your true self and to maintain your own voice.

Another important guideline for the essays: if you make a claim, back it up with evidence. What I mean is if you say you are something in your essay, make sure to have a real-life experience or accomplishment to exemplify what you are claiming. Don't just say you're a leader, talk about how you led certain groups and the impact you had on those groups. Don't just say you care about others, write about how you started a non-profit organization or charity group to benefit those in need. Ideally, you should not do much telling at all, just enough to make your claim clear. The majority of your essays should be *showing*, as in describing real-life things that you have actually done.

Now we'll move on to the next part of your senior year. Once you finish up your essays for your number one choice school, you need to begin working on the rest of the application. I will cover this topic in a later chapter called 'The Application'. For now, just continue with the senior year section.

Depending on the way your school works, your senior year academics will either be highly prioritized or not. Look at the deadline for when the Early Decision application is due for your first choice school. See if that deadline comes before or after the end of your first semester, first quarter, second quarter, first trimester, or whatever kind of system your school has. What you want to do is work just as hard on keeping your grades as high as you did junior year, up until you submit your application. For example, if your school finalizes report card grades after each quarter and you submit your Early Decision application slightly after the end of your second quarter, then you will want to keep on working your hardest (in terms of academics) until your second quarter grades are finalized. This is because you may need to report these grades to the first choice college and want them to be as high as possible. Once you have submitted the application, however, it is up to you whether or not you want to continue putting forth maximum academic effort. If you are highly confident that you will be accepted through Early Decision to the school you chose, then maybe you could lessen your academic intensity. If you do not plan on getting accepted, however, and still are applying to many other schools, then you may want to keep your grades as high as possible until you finish applying to all of your schools. In an ideal world you would keep the same intensity you had from junior year during senior year, but I know how it goes. You get tired and see how close you are, so it's hard to get the motivation to continue striving so fiercely. So, after you finish applying to all of your schools it is purely up to you to determine the amount of effort you want to put in. Be aware, though, that colleges have revoked acceptances (called rescission) in the past due to significant lowering of a student's grades. Keep this in mind if you decide to let up on the academics. I cannot promise you anything, but I would say that there is a safe zone of decrease in grades. If you have been a straight-A student all throughout high school, you can probably get away with a few B's and nothing less. I would not recommend receiving a grade that is more than one letter grade below what you normally receive. For example, if you normally get B's, do not get anything below a C. Since colleges do make you send your final and mid-year high school transcripts in, your senior grades do matter if you get accepted. The safest route to take would be to keep on trying your best, but I know that is not always feasible. You know yourself best: how confident you are that you will get accepted early, how many other schools you are applying to, and your own moral code.

In terms of extracurricular activities, you can actually stop doing some of them your senior year. Only quit activities once your application has been fully submitted, however, because that way you are not lying to colleges. If you say you are in debate, quit debate, and submit your application, *then you are lying to the university.* Do not lie to the university, it can only bring a lot of trouble into your life and other people's lives. If you want to quit something, do it after you have applied to all of your schools. Try not to quit too many of the activities you have been involved with, however, as it will look bad to your peers, teachers, and counselor. Often times these are the people either recommending you to colleges or electing you for leadership, so you generally do not want to do something that would make you look bad in their eyes. Luckily, however, if you followed this guide correctly you should be mostly participating in activities that you truly enjoy. Thus, the desire to quit a lot of your activities should not be present. If it is, fight it.

In summary of your senior year: generate a list of universities you will definitely apply to, identify your number one choice university, start your number one choice's essays as soon as possible (late summer), apply through your number one university's Early Decision program, continue applying to other schools, maintain or relax on academics, possibly abandon one or two groups max, and enjoy your final year of high school.

Chapter 6: What to do During Your Summers

Getting into an elite school does not only require effort during the academic school year. Your summers need to be spent wisely too if you want to have a shot. I should also mention, however, that the summer after your freshman year is not too big of a deal. Feel free to do as you wish this summer, as most colleges only care about your past two summers when you apply (sophomore to junior and junior to senior). Some of you reading this might feel disappointed that you can't spend your summers partying or laying by a pool, but if you pursue the right things, you can still enjoy your summer. The trick is to find a summer project/goal/mission that you can pursue that aligns well with what you are naturally interested in.

Summer time gives students a ton of time to essentially do whatever they want. Some work, some volunteer, some go on trips, and some don't do anything. You need to approach your summers slightly differently, however. Since you are trying to build an elite application, you need to partake in summer activities that relate to the other things you've built your application around during the school year. What I mean by this is that if you are really passionate about soccer, play on a nationally ranked team, captain of the team, and so on, then you need to find a summer activity that relates to soccer. This could be anything from starting a non-profit program that collects and donates soccer balls to kids in need around the world, working as a coach for inner-city high school kids, starting a local soccer camp, or whatever other ideas you can come up with. This is just one example. Basically, all you do

43

is take your interest and expand upon it during the summer by taking initiative and doing *something extra*. You also get bonus points to college admissions officers if you can relate your passion or interest to helping others. It may not be easy and may require tons of planning, but your choice of summer activity is what can separate you from the crowd. If you think about it, unless your summer activity is difficult or unique, there's a good chance that somebody else applying to the university has done the same thing. For example, if you went with your church on a mission trip to Haiti as just a regular volunteer, that's great, but it will not help you stand out in terms of college admissions. What would make this better is if you initiated, fund-raised for, and led the mission trip to Haiti that helped the natives in some way that relates to a passion of yours. For example, if you like to write, you could gather people to teach English and writing, or donate books. The point is to make sure that you summer activities are tailored to who you are and what you're interested in, as well as showing leadership and initiative.

Where this summer outline could go wrong, however, is if you need to work during the summer for financial reasons or your parents/guardians force you to work. I understand that not every student has the luxury of pursuing their passions during the summer. Some need to work at a stable job to help out the family, or for whatever other reasons. If this is the case, then I have two recommendations. First, you should try to find a job that somewhat relates to one of your passions. For example, if you like to dance competitively, try to find a job as a dance instructor. If you like computer programming, maybe you could work as a freelance developer. It is possible to make money from your passion at a young age, you just need to do your research and get creative. If this does not work out for you, however, and your left to the typical low-skill, high-schooler job, then I still have some tips for you. You can take the entry-level job, but work your absolute hardest at it and treat your supervisors, co-workers, and customers with the utmost respect and kindness. You need to be the hardest working employee where you work and have your bosses and co-workers think very highly of you. Then, once it comes time to apply to colleges, you should ask for a letter of recommendation from the boss or supervisor who you think thinks the most highly of you. This way when college admissions officers read this, they can at least see that you treated the job very seriously and that you have great character. On top of this, it would be ideal if you wrote just a little bit in your application somewhere about why you had to work during the summer instead of pursuing your passions. This way admissions officers will be more understanding of your situation and you could even make yourself look better to them if you play your cards right. For example, if your family needed the additional income during the summer for financial reasons, and you got a glowing hot letter of recommendation from your supervisor at work, then admissions officers could very well look favorably upon your summer spent working. It could make them see your integrity, grit, and amazing personal character. Thus, even if you can't do any of the summer activities I recommended earlier, you still have (possibly just as good of) options to pursue.

In terms of when to pursue these endeavors, I recommend that you space it out between your two summers before graduation. Optimally, you should pursue one project/goal/endeavor after your sophomore year and then another after your junior year. If you wish, however, you can do things in whatever order you want. You could wait until the summer before your senior year to pursue multiple endeavors if you wish, as long as you make sure that they are going to be effective pursuits in the long-run.

In summary of this chapter: spend your summers wisely, pursue a summer endeavor that relates to one of your passions that you have already been pursuing in high school, if you cannot pursue a passion then work your hardest at a summer job, make sure your activity shows leadership and initiative, do something unique and tailored to you, and get ready to write about your summer experiences in your application.

Chapter 7: The Application

Now that you've done all of the work, it's time to showcase it. The actual college application itself, in my humble opinion, is as *equally as important* as the actual accomplishments you have achieved over the years. You *must* showcase yourself effectively if you want to gain admission to an elite school.

The first step to writing a bomb application is to think about all of the activities and accomplishments you have been involved with or won. Now, try to identify a common relation between all of those things and develop an overarching theme to your high school experience. For example, you could develop your application around computer programming and entrepreneurship. If you have gone to hackathons, released an app, built websites, done freelance work, or built a tech business, then you have a lot to write about come application time! Include these achievements in your essays and use them as subtle evidence of your entrepreneurial spirit, initiative, and passion for programming. Don't just list your accomplishments on your application, also write about them. Use the essays as space to not only talk about your personal values and story, but intertwine your accomplishments too. Write about why you accomplished what you did and why you enjoy doing what you do. Make sure to use your accomplishments and activities as evidence of what and who you say you are. Much like how a research paper needs evidence, so do your college essays. The evidence, however, is not a scientific fact, but instead, an achievement or involvement of yours.

Going back to the earlier example, if your application's themes are computer programming and entrepreneurship, then stick to those! Do not spend too much time writing about how you like to sail as a hobby and how you once volunteered at a medical hospital. Sure, it's fine to mention things like this briefly, but do not give them too much space in your application. Remember, application space is precious and needs to be filled with only things that will be effective. If you played for one of your high school's sports teams, played on the band, or something similar that took a lot of your time, however, don't be afraid to mention it. I would recommend just mentioning it in your list of activities, though, and not in your essays. Colleges do like to see that you aren't just a working machine and do some things for fun, so it can be beneficial to list one or two activities that stray from your theme that you did just for fun in high school. Moreover, this is only one example of how a cohesive application could be built. First and foremost, your application needs to be built around you and what you have done. Not what you think the school wants. What elite schools want is a diverse body of students, not a bunch of students who are 'okay' at many things and great at none. A school can achieve diversity of the student body through accepting high school students who have each shown themselves to be good at different things. Everyone has talents, inclinations, and interests: use yours. Of course, you need good grades and test scores, but outside of that you have a lot of freedom to develop yourself and your application however you want. Just make sure that you enjoy what you are doing, try your hardest at it, and really explain your activities well in your application.

On a final note about your application, please make sure to effectively convey a theme. Your application must show who you are (or at least who you think you are) at 18 years old. You must have at least one theme in your application, and should have no more than three. The ideal number of themes would be two. Your two themes can be anything from leadership and business to chemistry and research, just as long as it is true to you. Just like when you write a research essay that has a theme, the theme is not the only thing you write about in the essay, but it is the central tying knot that holds your essay together. A strong research essay is not just a bunch of unrelated evidence and claims, but a cohesive argument. The same goes for your application, except you are arguing yourself to the university.

Chapter 8: Good-to-Know Things

Now that you've completely read about all four years of high school, you should be able to have a better idea of what it takes to gain acceptance into a university of elite caliber and how you as an individual can do it. This chapter is going to just be about miscellaneous tips and information that I found useful in the past, and thought you might as well. Some of the tips will be related and some will not be. Essentially, they are just here to help give you that extra edge as you go through high school and the college application process.

- For studying for the SAT, I recommend pairing the *SAT Prep Black Book* with the latest *Official SAT Study Guide*. For studying for the ACT, I recommend pairing the *ACT Prep Black Book* with the latest *Official ACT Prep Guide*.

- Check if the university you are applying to requires AP scores to be sent to them. If you have less than perfect scores, or scores that you do not think will help your application, then simply don't send them. Some universities have a policy, however, that frowns upon students who do not send in AP scores. Watch out for this.

- Check if the university you are applying to requires all standardized test scores to be sent, or only a single one. If only a single one is required, then only send in your best score. Even though some universities will say that they don't require all of your scores, but recommend sending all of them in and will only take your best score, do not trust them. Only send in your best score, as long as it does not break any of their university rules.

- As you go throughout high school, keep a running-list of all the activities and accomplishments you have done or are doing. Write them all down and separate them by year. This way when it comes to to apply to colleges, you have a comprehensive list of everything you have done and can easily pull from it.

- Never burn bridges with people. For those of you who don't fully understand what this saying means, it means to not end contact with someone on a bad note. Do all that you can in your power to maintain a healthy and positive relationship with everyone you interact with. Whether this interaction be with your peer, teacher, boss, or whoever else, make sure it ends on a positive note. You never know how they can come back to assist or bite you in the future.

- Try not to talk so much about how you plan on attending an elite university. It is in bad taste. It will make many people dislike you, which is not an enjoyable life to live.

- When deciding whether or not to take the ACT or the SAT, there is a trick to help you decide. Try to find out which test has been most commonly taken by admitted students in the past at the specific schools you are applying to. This information could be found on the university's website or by calling someone who works at the university's admissions office. As of when I wrote this, most of the individuals accepted into Ivy League schools take the SAT.

- Although this tip is not necessary, you could use it if you think it would benefit you. If you are struggling with your G.P.A. in high school, or confused on how high your G.P.A. should be, there is a way you can get somewhat of a G.P.A. range you should be aiming for. If the college you desire releases data about the most recently admitted class, then search if they release that class's average high school G.P.A. Not all university's release this data, so don't bank on finding it. If you do get lucky, however, and find this data, then take a look at the average accepted high school G.P.A. A good range to aim to graduate high school with then would be about .1 higher or .1 lower than this average.

- Lastly, do not look down on other people for setting goals to get into less selective schools than you have, and do not think you are a better person than someone simply because of the school you are going to. Be proud of what you have and what you aim to accomplish, but also know that everyone deserves respect.

Chapter 9: Final Remarks

You've made it all the way through the end of this book and now should have the information you need to guide you along your journey to your dream school. This book cannot give or guarantee success, but what it can do is give you the knowledge you need to succeed. Now that you know what needs to be done, it is time for you to apply what you have learned.

The journey will be tough. Gaining acceptance into an elite university is not an easy task for anybody, but it can pay off more than one can even imagine in the future. Having access to the countless opportunities, being surrounded by incredibly intelligent individuals, and walking through life with an elite certification are only some of the limitless number of benefits from attending an elite university.

What I can guarantee is the fact that if I can do it, so can you. I had no incredibly exceptional talents in high school, but I did work very hard and meticulously. I planned well and executed well. I hope that you see from reading this guide how intricate, yet possible, the process is for gaining admittance to an elite school. You don't need to have done world-renowned research and you don't need to be the absolute best at something. All you need is some belief in yourself, a long-term plan, and the courage to pursue your dreams.

Made in the USA
Middletown, DE
13 October 2018